HOLY GHOST TOWN

Also by Tim Sherry

Micopacen (chapbook)
One of Seven Billion

HOLY GHOST TOWN

POEMS BY

TIM SHERRY

Tim Sherry

*To Marion,
With hope that you
enjoy the poems -- and that
someday you visit
Holden.
Tim*

Published by

CIRQUE PRESS

Sandra Kleven — Michael Burwell
3978 Defiance Street
Anchorage, AK 99504

cirquepressaknw@gmail.com
www.cirquejournal.com

Cover: *Summer Jubilee, or Skipping Vespers* by Kristen Gilje
Author photo by Peter Serko
Book Design by Nora Gecan, Graphic Designer and Art Director

Print ISBN 9781073735242

To all those who believe there is
more to wilderness than trees

Acknowledgments

Thanks to Holden Village for its inclusion in a 2010 newsletter the poem "Garbage In" and on its website in 2010 the poem "Arrival."

"Sometimes All You Can Do Is Just Wonder" appeared in *Seminary Ridge Review* in 2012 and in the 2014 full-length poetry collection *One of Seven Billion* from Moonpath Press.

"Dish Team!" appeared in *Rattle* in 2014 under the title "Dish Team at Church Camp."

"Shadow of My Father" was included in *One of Seven Billion*.

"Ice Cream at Church Camp" appeared in the 2017 anthology *Ice Cream Poems: reflections on life with ice cream* from World Enough Writers, an imprint of Concrete Wolf Press.

Special thanks to the Artsmith Artist Residency where some of the first poems for *Holy Ghost Town* were born during a residency in 2010.

Much of the historical information and "The Last Letter and the Reply" is from Charles P. Lutz's 1987 book *Surprising Gift: The Story of Holden Village, Church Renewal Center.*

The term *holy ghost town* is taken from an area newspaper article at the time that ownership of the abandoned mine and town was transferred by the Howe Sound mining company to the Lutheran Bible Institute.

HOLY GHOST TOWN

Introduction

At the end of an eleven mile road up Railroad Creek from Lake Chelan in the North Cascade Mountains of Washington State, the Howe Sound Company operated the Holden Mine from 1937 until 1957.

It was one of the largest copper, gold, silver, and zinc mines of its day, and the four hundred miners and their families who worked the mine lived there in a company town consisting of a dining hall, a hotel, a hospital, a cafe, a recreation center, a school, a post office, dormitories for the single miners, a hundred single family homes for married miners, shops and maintenance buildings, and fourteen chalet homes for administrative staff and their families.

When the price of copper dropped in the 1950s, the mine closed. And because of its remote location in the wilderness, the Howe Sound Company simply walked away leaving in place everything—all the buildings, vehicles, equipment, records and papers—everything.

Dishes were left on tables. The pins were left standing in the bowling alley. The barber shop ready for the next haircut, the pool hall with balls and cue sticks on the tables, the dining hall tables and chairs—all left.

A year later, crews tried to salvage some of the material from the mine buildings, but gave up when it was not profitable. Power lines had been removed. Refuse and debris had been buried in the mile of tailings. The mine shaft was left open.

For two years the town of Holden stood empty. Some speculated that it might make a good resort. Logging operations were discussed. The US Forest Service, whose land the town stood on, weighed in. Then in 1960, through a series of events that might be called serendipity, the mining company, after three years of letters from someone named Wesley H. Prieb, simply gave the mine and the buildings of the town, for one dollar, to the Lutheran Bible Institute (LBI) in Seattle to be used for what Wesley H. Prieb had proposed to be a church summer youth camp.

Two of the letters are dated serendipitously April 1—a notion that seems to have ended up as part of what is today Holden Village, with close ties to the Lutheran church a year-round Christian retreat center whose stated core values are worship, theology, hospitality, vocation, diversity, grace, shalom, ecology, gifts, study, rest, place, community, and *hilarity*.

The village needed much help after it was acquired by LBI, and in 1961 students came to Holden to clean up, do repairs, and make the buildings livable. At the same time, volunteers worked to restore power, make the dining hall usable, and repair vehicles left behind.

In the summer of 1962, the village opened to the public. For the next fifty years, it operated each summer with a hundred staff to host two to three hundred guests per week who came to the town of Chelan, got on a boat to the old community of Lucerne where Railroad Creek meets Lake Chelan, and then rode on reclaimed school buses eleven miles into the mountains to Holden.

During its first years, even though much was done to clear the area around the mine of debris, remove buildings, and close the mine shaft to entry, there was great concern at Holden about the water filled with heavy metals coming from the mile of tailings and the mine portal—that over time contaminated Railroad Creek so that it was dead to any life.

Finally, in the early 2000s serious discussion resumed to decide what to do to capture the contaminated water, route it to a water treatment plant, and send it, cleaned, back into the river—so that the two miles of river that had been dead for decades could again sustain life. And again a kind of serendipity happened when the federal government mandated that a multinational mining company, the Rio Tinto Group, bore responsibility to pay for the work.

Starting in 2013, work began. Because the village had to be closed to visitors in order to house the mine remediation workers, Holden was able to do the work to upgrade the electrical, sewage, and fire protection systems as well as improve walkways, roads, bridges, and relocate the site for recycling, the wood yard, the buildings for vehicle maintenance and storage, the Hike Haus, and create a new site for the village museum torn down to allow for new roads.

After four years of mine remediation work, the village re-opened to visitors in 2017. And even though much was done to make it a safer and more accessible place, Holden Village still looks like and has the feel of an old mining town in the wilderness.

The Last Letter and the Reply

April 1, 1960 letter to:

Howe Sound Company
Chelan, Washington

Dear Mr. Roper,

I am writing to inquire about the status of Holden Village at Chelan, Washington. I believe that this property might be a desirable place for the use of the church or the Lutheran Bible Institute as a summer camp. The church needs a camp which could be used for our young people.

Information pertaining to the price presently being asked, the status or any other information will be deeply appreciated.

Thank you for your kind help and information.

Very sincerely yours,
Wesley H. Prieb

1960 telegram to:

Wesley H. Prieb
Lutheran Bible Institute, Seattle

YOUR LETTER RECEIVED. PLEASE CALL OUR OFFICE SALT LAKE CITY COLLECT. MR. KIRKLAND, MAGNUM, UTAH

A.G. Kirkland
Magnum, Utah

The Poems

If ever we understood this place, we'd spoil it!

—Hortie Christman, at Holden
from 1965 to 1973, known as
the patron saint of volunteers

PROLOGUE

Holy Ghost Town

Closing the Holden mine had gone on for weeks
as rumors whispered in the dining hall
and down through the shafts. The tailings left
their orange dust in places that had been let go.
Bears sniffed something wrong
in houses standing empty here and there.
The trucks parked more than they rolled.

The last day as a mine and a town came
the way sudden death and miracles happen.
Just like that. Everyone left except a caretaker
to jiggle the last padlock. When he checked
in his rearview mirror, the buildings must have looked
like a Lincoln Log town finally finished
on Christmas morning with everyone off to Grandma's.

Hikers coming through wondered at the ghost town.
Vandals broke windows and left graffiti.
The mining company worked its other mountains.
A year later, a newspaper story that the whole place
was for sale shook old heads in bars
down the lake. Some folks from back east
traveled out for a look and thought maybe a resort.

When a kid named Wes Prieb read the story,
he thought, *Hmmm*, and wrote to the company
offering a Biblical idea. Why not a church camp?
A reduced price? A miracle? A sort of seminarian
at a Bible school in Seattle, what was he thinking?
The idea couldn't have a ghost of a chance.
But why not—seriously—when it's just sitting there?

After three years of back and forth letters,
something Old Testament happened.
The company offered to give the whole thing away.
When Wes told everyone, they wondered if it might be
an April Fools joke. But finally they had to believe
that God must have been out walking in his wilderness
and decided to make Holden a *holy* ghost town.

July above Lake Chelan
in Washington State's
North Cascade Mountains

COMING IN

Everybody needs beauty as well as bread, places to play in and pray in, where nature may heal and give strength to body and soul.

—John Muir

On the Way Up Lake

Water as clear as the meaning
of wildflowers that stair step
from high mountain meadows
down to Lake Chelan
marks the equation
between altitude and depth.

At Sanctuary Cove,
The Lady of the Lake slows
to give passengers a closer look
at barcode in the rock
that tells of millennia, like centuries
told in the rings of cut trees.

Above Domke Falls,
mountain goats
demonstrate balance
where Satan would never have dared
take Jesus
to show him promises.

What does he mean,
the boat captain saying
that the bottom of the lake is so cold
fish don't try to live
at depths no soundings
have really measured?

The peaks looking down on the dock
at Lucerne steward their snow
into enough cascade
to protect wildflowers from burning
in the heat of summer and to keep
the lake as deep as faith needs.

Whitecaps rip along past the boat.
Altitude and depth
equal balance just as surely
as sin and salvation at Holden
balance between
forever and ever, Amen.

Arrival

There are still names for places in the road
from decades ago when trucks rumbled ore
to Lake Chelan. Today it's a reclaimed school bus
up the switchbacks, through the narrows,
onto the flat that means *soon there.*
Words for wilderness speak from the seats.
Pine. Granite. Peak. Waterfall! Bear?
Then right at the road is a mile of burned trees.
The driver explains to the rear-view mirror
how fire is the way the forest *re-seeds* itself.

Or did he say *recedes*? In the silence of awe,
we give thanks that we weren't here the years
the forest on fire took back. As the ride turns
into just a ride for the last mile, we know
either word means more than the driver is telling us.
Isn't it why we came? We want to see the forest
and the trees. We want new growth. We want
a place where meaning is more than words.
Finally we round the last turn into the village
where *Welcome!* waits underneath the waving.

The driver stops, stands, and explains wilderness
using sacred words, as if in prayer.
Then he drives us ahead to our week of mountains.
We step off, nervous at the applause and hyperbole
shouted by those waiting to greet us. We wonder
what kind of place is this, this old mining town
that dug into the mountain and shipped its ore
to the smelter in Tacoma where it melted
into our abundant lives, lives so in need
of a fire we hope still burns low inside us.

Orientation

The spirits told of in legends
before prospecting brought the miners in
are still here. Ten thousand years of wilderness
doesn't give up. Its gods
are flood and avalanche, wind and fire.

And this old mining town is full of its own ghosts
that refuse to leave. No Stephen King convolutions
hide them. No Dickens plot brings them out.
A speed limit sign and no cars,
an empty barber shop are incarnation.

The bowling alley's fourth lane
must symbolize something beyond Trinity
that came before the twenty years of copper.
A picture in the museum tells the story
of college kids who seeded this place with holiness.

The hundred homes of Winston Camp, burned
to remove temptation, are gone to trees and brush
with only bulkheads and foundations left
to imagine lives there. The baseball field
has lost its dreams, but its mention still turns heads

on the trail up the valley. There never was a railroad,
but the creek that is a river is ghosted with that name.
Trucks rumbling ore to the lake, conversation
in the dining hall after the second shift,
arithmetic in the schoolhouse still echo—

and echo anew when the bus brings in new villagers,
when a baby cries in the night and a dad takes her
out to the porch to rock through it, when Narnia
chatters with running and paint on the floor.
The mine and its town were left behind—

and now each day, each week, through the seasons,
Holden Village gives name, adds a chapter,
brings new life to a place that died
and stayed right where it always was—in a paradise
full of old spirits, the Holy Ghost, and wilderness.

A Good Story

The multinational Rio Tinto Group
was mandated to pay for the work
to clean up the Holden mine site.

To repair damage done to Railroad Creek
by heavy metal in water coming from
the Holden mine, that kind of repair
would cost more than anyone could afford.
So it took not just anyone. And after
fifty years of stabs at it by the county,
the state, the feds, serendipity echoed—

as if Wes Prieb had written more letters.

Rio Tinto's 500 million dollars was red tape
cut through, a magic wand waved,
prayers answered as Holden once again
housed men working on Copper Mountain.
It was called *remediation* to give the river
back to the fish; but history now tells
the story as faith and wilderness renewed.

First Night at Vespers

Vespers is mantra each evening with music
to pick you up, bad jokes to bring the Good News,
and familiar words to fill cracks
in the life you brought because you heard
that Holden is a place like no other—
where Bible is sometimes so camp
it doesn't hurt to laugh a little,
and where your name is spoken
your first night and every day, every day.
Along with the new arrivals
you are introduced and stand up.
Six degrees of separation sits right beside you
and tonight someone will want to know
if you are from . . . and want to talk.

The old gymnasium configured into sanctuary
plays along. It invites you to find
yourself in the story painted on its ceiling
with the same sit and stare as in Rome.
It teases you to come and go
thinking of what to reap and sow.
Looking around, you know
what the word *welcome* really means.
In the sermon, you hear a story that needs
the Holy Ghost to be true. You are told
this is a place where you can come to Jesus
and laugh at what you have always taken
so seriously. You understand better
why God pays attention to sparrows.

Ice Cream at Church Camp

There's no ice in the New Testament.
So standing in line after vespers,
waiting the opening of the snack shop,
the question is so church camp
when someone wonders
if Jesus would have served ice cream
for dessert at the Last Supper—
had there been such a thing in his day.
It's more of the silliness
that sometimes seems so gospel
in the mountains
where such questions
are refrigerated most of the year
under ten feet of snow—
and deciding in the heat
of a summer evening
which flavor, cone or dish,
how many scoops, is just as important
as answering, *What would Jesus do?*

The Children, Themselves

A hundred children
make Holden a small town again.
They come for the week with mom and dad
to mine the good old days
still here in the mountains.

It's summer vacation back in Indiana,
but here it's still themselves to learn.
And school here is children's songs in Narnia.
It's helping with dish team.
It's a basketball game before vespers
calling your own fouls.
It's along trails that lead back
to the pool hall and snack shop
at the end of every day.
Sometimes at night, porches teach
teenagers the tenderness of touching.

By Tuesday afternoon each new week,
everyone knows who fits where,
and the good old days
break out in a water fight
with garden hoses and balloons.

They promise to be back for dinner.
But from the time of breakfast,
every day the children are out and gone—
with the run of a place we used to call home.

Degrees of Separation

A first name and a smile sitting down
starts the conversation. *From where?* is next.
Then it's twenty minutes of geography.
In Jesus' time, it was easier—maybe three degrees
separating the world around the Mediterranean
where villages the size of Holden were big places,
and Rome was New York.

Tonight it's eight people at the table
from all over the Bible
hoping to find someone who knows someone
who reads parables the same as they.
If not parables to connect them, then stories
about someone who knows someone
who went to the same school
or traveled to the same place last summer.
Everyone wants to know, *How long are you here?*
which leads to, *What brings you to Holden?*

That last part of it separates
the one at the end of the table
who gets up to put his dishes away,
to walk out into the evening, and stand alone
down by the river. The story to be told about him
would have been parable
had his name come up at Jesus' table.

Grace

Grace comes into the village
on the noon bus.
The people gathered wave
and applaud those stepping off
as if they are dignitaries.
They do it for everyone,
the little girl is reassured.
But she has been teased
all her life, and hesitates before
stepping down onto the roadway.

She had felt the same at recess,
in the neighborhood, even
Sunday school. In the school play,
when she forgot her song,
the sixth-grade boys laughed,
gave her mock applause, and hooted
her name to let her know
that a fifth-grade girl
with a grandma name like that
is supposed to know the words.

Walking from the bus,
big *HELLOS* greet her, and a boy—
a boy!—holds up a sign
with her name painted in big letters
with flowers around it
and *Welcome!* underneath.
At ten going on eleven,
she doesn't know very much
about her name; but on that sign,
it is who she is at Holden.

Hiking In from the West Side

It was our fourth day on the trail
from Darrington across to Holden Village.
We had plenty of time to make it
by sunset if we picked up the pace.
But after three more hours,
the young woman from work
who had asked to join us *three old guys*
she had joked when she asked,
noticed we were past our prime
and pretended she needed to stop.
We were at Hart Lake where day hikers
had come up from Holden
for their two hours and lunch.
Some were swimming just down the lake
from where we stopped,
and the young woman with us
decided a quick dip would be fun.
We were polite as she stripped down
to panties and the just-a-tee-shirt
we had pretended not to notice
as she was getting into her sleeping bag
the last three nights. All of a sudden
a plane was overhead from the west,
which you don't see very often
coming down a North Cascade valley.
Everyone along the lake looked up
and waved. The young woman, too,
stood up out of the water and waved,
longer than anyone after she noticed
we were watching her and not the plane—
maybe because she thought it would help us
pick up the pace if she stood there waving.

Garbage In

Garbage is treasure
where there is no landfill,
no truck at the curb on Tuesdays.
There is no place in the wilderness
for it, and the village that is Holden
saves it. In the costume shop,
old clothes and trinkets
are stashed for children
to raid for dress-up days.
Potty Patrol is a place
for lost and found stuff
that has to have a name
with enough tease for the taking.
Food and trash are a movie star,
and *garbo* is sorted for burning,
compost, or landfill down the lake
on a barge. Even an old joke
is good for another laugh because
everything is worth something.
Wilderness is too sacred
for even a candy wrapper
not to be picked up; and the village
is full of too much holiness
for the same not to happen
when someone fallen arrives.

No Comforts of Home

You've come to Holden knowing
you will share a room, walk down the hall
to *Men* and *Women* across from each other,
share a shower with fifteen or twenty people.

When you arrive at Lodge 2, Room 5, you have to
make up the bed yourself. Communal living
doesn't describe you in your underwear
forgetting to close the door the first night.

Asking the couple on the porch who have
been here for two weeks is how you know
who it is in Room 11 with the crying baby.
Your closet has wire hangers from 1967.

Asking someone for soap you forgot to bring
from home isn't asking for charity you are told;
It's the New Testament, the woman in 7
jokes when she gives you her extra bar.

Suddenly awakened, you hear the young couple
next door honeymooning at midnight.
You don't need the alarm clock you brought
with the five a.m. four-year-old upstairs.

But after a week of greetings every morning,
and goodnights from new friends
you've made, here you don't need
the four bedrooms and three baths back home.

The Buses

Hilarity is part of its core values,
and buses are part of the laughter
that is part of the story of Holden.
Their names—*Chelan, Jubilee, Entiat,*
North Star, Honey, Pookie, Tuque—
all come from years of crawling guests
up the switchbacks from the lake
and then the slow half hour into the village.

They needed names for the staff to decide
whose turn it was each day
to meet the fast boat and then the slow boat,
who would need a few days off for repairs,
who to park in the fall as the number
of guests coming in needed just one bus.

All still yellow from their school bus days,
but covered in eleven miles of dirt road
twice a day, the buses are Holden's way
of starting guests off with a chuckle
that they are not back in elementary school,
but they are on their way to a place
where what is important in the wilderness
is often as simple as the names of things.

It might make one wonder that if
there had been buses in Jesus' day,
he might have called them James and John,
Andrew, Philip and Bartholomew, Peter,
without a doubt Thomas—and then sent them
out to pick up anyone wishing to get on.

LOOK! LOOK! LOOK!

God writes the Gospel not in the Bible alone, but also on trees, and in the flowers and clouds and stars.
—Martin Luther

Up Early

City time goes on even without alarm clocks
when light behind the mountains
and birdsong through the open window wake me.
Lying quietly is no way to start a day
at a church camp, and I decide a cup of coffee
in the dining hall and a walk along the river.
      A different time goes on
      down from the glaciers,
      ahead where a deer drinks,
      over the mountains
      as the sun pinks the sky.
What the clock says doesn't matter.
The only one up isn't loneliness.
This early doesn't need God yet.
An hour of walking alone in the wilderness
in such morning light, around the next bend
I imagine myself right at heaven's door.

At Winston Camp

The walk to the site of the miners' houses
cuts through the growth of seven decades.
The trees alone would have been enough,
but time needed more to cover where
the hundred homes of Winston Camp were.
There. No there. And here, where a bulkhead
runs beside the road gone back to grass.

After the mine was closed
and everyone just walked away,
the Forest Service burned the homes—
to protect the forest from fire
the reports said. Irony didn't matter.
The real truth is empty buildings
stand in the way of wilderness wanting back.

But towns left suddenly can't take all their ghosts
with them. Looking for anything more
than wilderness, I stop to poke a toe
at a hammer head. A rubber hose isn't a snake
after a few minutes of clearing brush away.
A half hour later I'm still digging, hoping
to find something of what is gone still here.

The Mountains' Secrets

Easy to know, hard to understand,
the mountains are their own poetry
where no words mean more
than conversation to keep the trail
in front of me. Up there
above the highest peaks where glaciers
and snow keep their cold secrets,
the circling bird is too small
against the sunrise to be an eagle.
Here on the trail, we are too small
to be a Muir or the Yakama who
may or may not have come this way.
This then. The mountains
are enough left of Eden, and this trail
is someone's idea of a way
for one like me to know a little
of what I will never understand.

Mine Remediation

The spirits whispered warning
that treasure taken from a mountain
creates a *forever*. And after fifty years
the rest of forever needed a fix.

No commandment stopped
metal and water from mixing,
turning toxic, then finding gravity
down to the river. No policy
governed the wind working tailings
into dust as orange as fire.

The mine could not be put back
in the mountain,
though forgiveness had been asked
for decades after the digging stopped.
Finally, statute and standards
had to heal the wilderness

for wind to blow free of dust again,
for water to flow as in psalm,
for eagles to fish the river
another ten thousand years.

Wilderness Perspective

The mountains up the valley
re-position their peaks
on the horizon after glacier melt.

Flood and avalanche
carve the slopes while
tectonic plates work the depths.

I walk the trail
to check off that I came through—
pretending my footprints
or a branch broken off
will be noted too
as God tends to the sparrows.

But the mountains go on
in their disregard for anything
less than millennium.

The wind stirs.
Leaves and dust blow across
the trail behind me.

Mountain Lake Traiku

The summer sunrise
takes its time, and the mountains
shoot light back at the moon.

At Hart Lake, the flies,
too lazy in the morning,
forget there are fish.

Flies and fish and light
dance until the lake and wind
decide just the light.

Back from Holden Lake

At dinner, telling of the day's hike
we fail when we try to describe
sitting on the shore of the lake.
The hour we spent
with our sandwiches and fruit
just looking up
needs more vocabulary
than words.
The bear that wandered by
is the only sentence
that makes eye contact.
The rest is too close to the sky
that was the water that was the sky.

Fire

Clouds over the Cascades
and the weather report pinned up
at the dining hall doors are not July.

Black at night and blue all day
are the only colors expected in the sky
in any 24 hours of summer.

But gray coming east
this morning sends rumors
through the village.

Thunder speeds the talk of rain,
and lightning. Worry turns
from hikes postponed to what if fire;

and at the start of lunch
there are reminders of what to do
if evacuation orders come.

But nothing is said
of what it means if wilderness
burns itself so red the sky is gone.

Afternoon in the Village Museum

Miner league baseball here lasted twenty years,
and then church camp slow pitch petered on
in the '60s and '70s with pick-up games
where anyone could play. Finally
it wasn't hoot and holler enough to walk the mile
up to the ball field, and the last game there
hovers somewhere back in the '80s of stories.

The diamond is long gone—first to tall grass
and brush, then a prayer maze,
finally during mine remediation
bulldozed level as a place to park excavators.
All the games the miners played
are now just pictures in the museum—
of baseball—and of basketball and bowling—
pictures of miners wanting their bragging rights
the same as anyone in St. Louis or Brooklyn.

From the looks on their black and white faces,
the air was thin enough here in the mountains
for them to believe every ball and strike
was World Series, every strike and spare
was Friday night after work on the line,
every lay-up with two seconds showing
was the championship of the world.

All Living Creatures

At Holden, a bird building a nest
at the river finds an immortality
twig by twig more
than any prayers can answer.

Chipmunks stealing crumbs
from lunch taken outside
need no blessing
on their communion with hunger.

Deer, come to the village
just as vespers sings our last song,
search clover in the lawn
where it is field enough as if heaven.

When we arrive, we may not know
much of what to expect;
but we know when we leave
how much is not needed for salvation.

The Right Word

Do I dare use another paradise word
for such a place as Holden,
to be just more cliché
about a million years of wilderness
still clinging to the mountains?
Even King James must have worried
about Eden in translation.

The dining hall
is where I hear the right word
when a little girl running through,
holding wildflowers
brought back from the day's hike,
shouts it over and over,
Look! Look! Look!

Imagine If Chief Joseph Came

Imagine if Chief Joseph came to teach at Holden.
He might invite the villagers to sit down
with him on the lawn on Chalet Hill. There
he might talk of spirits that made the world
and live on in old stories and in the wind
that cools the wilderness in August.
There might be long silences so that
questions without answers might be answered.

The wilderness might whisper questions
about all its work to come back
after copper and trucks. Chief Joseph
might lean in to hear, and talk of wounds
that take history to heal. He might lean back
and look up at Buckskin Mountain for answers
that only water and rocks can give.
Mine remediation might be explained that way.

The spirits might stay an hour.
They might come and go during that time.
The villagers who were invited
might miss dinner, might sit far into the night.
Chief Joseph might stay as long
as they have questions.
He might answer how he could be at Holden
and no more forever in the wind.

Backsliding at Church Camp

The rules expect attendance at vespers,
and you always follow the rules religiously.
But here, the wilderness you came for
is out there—and on your way
to the village center where the Gospel gathers,
a deer on the road just past the last lodge
turns and seems to say, *Come.* Your hesitation
is a ten second prayer asking forgiveness,
and you go. At a turn a mile down the road,
a sign that marks the start of a trail
also seems to say, *Come*—and you head up
to a place among the trees
where silence is unspoken parable.

WILDERNESS PILGRIMS

Sky over endless mountains. All the junk that goes with being human drops away . . .

—Gary Snyder in "Piute Creek"

Dish Team!

Dish team isn't washing feet
bowed before the shamed and poor.
It isn't getting anyone to heaven
because of its goodness.
The dirty side is the plates and pans
coming at you like Lucy's chocolates
and staying just behind enough
to keep up. Human frailty itself.
The clean side is sanitized hands
touching only the things ready to put away
that come out hot! from the big dishwasher
someone named *Aunt Alice*. Purity of spirit.

Shouting *Hallelujah!* is the new guy's idea
of Trinity involved in doing dishes.
If only it was that way at home.
Here it's part of the deal for staff
who volunteer—room and board
for the summer to work garbage, plumbing,
lawns and gardens, child care, anything
needed to keep thy neighbor—
and then everyone does dish team
once a week to seal the covenant.

At home it's a chore
just to load the dishwasher every day.
At Holden, it's dish team!
for two hours after every meal
with the Father one hour,
the Son another hour, and the Holy Ghost
whooping it up until the last dish is done.

Ghosts in the Night

At Holden, every villager is a walking ghost
after the light has dropped west.
Familiar faces of the week
come down the road leaning their heads
together as if to keep secret their talk.
I think back to the family picnics
we had when uncles did the same
so we couldn't hear the jokes
they told. It was at the time of day
when there was too little dark to hide them,
but no one could read their lips.

There are jokes told here too

that need the evening for protection—
when the Gospel is no picnic.
Vespers tonight was all about God
doing things that don't make sense,
like showing up as Jesus and then
disappearing. So what else is there to do
but laugh and walk off into the night
hoping the Holy Ghost is out there
somewhere in the wilderness,
not making much sense either,
but listening to our lips move?

The Bell

The village bell is country church, town center,
one room school, all day long to remind us
of everything from breakfast to vespers.
Today it rings a famous piano player in
on the noon bus. His dress shoes and sport coat
don't fit the gear of the village.
His hair is city cut. He carries a briefcase.
On the day's schedule he is the evening concert.
At dinner he sits alone, and those who don't know
wonder if he is from the board of directors.

After vespers he waits off to the side, patient
until the hymnals are put away. Those who stayed
move to the best seats. A boy is told to go
and ring the bell to hurry everyone back
who may have forgotten or gone for ice cream.
Someone announces *The* who he is
and he sits down to play a different kind of sacred.
In the audience, just arrived from Minnesota,
Grand piano? In the Mountains? Then, *Ragtime?*
The big grand dances Fats Waller,
Scott Joplin, Jelly Roll Morton where we've heard
nothing but hymns the past week.

The third number in, tapping feet
can't help but pray along as he plays those keys
into wildfire and roaring wind, avalanche—
music rolling out the open door to celebrate
the night the same way a bell keeping time between
sunrise and sunset rings true in the wilderness.

I Am at Holden

This may be a prayer as I go back to my room
after morning Bible study and leaf through
the Old Testament wondering about all the things
holy there. But it's in the Commandments
to have no other gods than the one handing down
the rules. I don't want this to sound like the poems
of Jim Harrison about the rivers of Montana
and the upper peninsula of Michigan
where the stars or a good beer are divine, or like
any of the songs of the Cheyenne about spirits
in the wind through the trees and prairie grass.

But if a prayer does what it is supposed to do,
get you to a place where you have all the help
you need and gives answers to the big questions—
like why we are here, who made this world—
then I have to wonder why we've glorified
so many things and then made them into gods.

If humans can imagine it and then do it,
fly and fix hearts and tell rivers where to run,
make Dick Tracy's watch really talk,
if doctors can bring people back to life in the ICU
and chemistry make composites
stronger than diamonds, if it seems we have
godlike powers to make the world in our own image,
maybe the Old Testament missed something.
Is what we dream closer than we think
to heaven? The sparrow dead yesterday on the trail,
is our noting it more than paying attention?

Who is it we see in the mirror in the morning?
Is the image there Genesis 1:27?
Maybe the very God who set it in stone
on his mountain answered my prayer
when he showed up and told Moses his name,
I am that I am. Maybe at Holden I am too.

Meditations on Coffee

I.
Lining the shelf in the dining hall
are six giant coffee makers—
two sets of three in a row
connected by pipes and valves
left from the mining days when
24/7 needed a thousand cups a day
to keep the ore on schedule.
The three-in-a-row back then
weren't anything close
to what we might joke as Trinity
at Holden today.
Their name told the schedule
they kept—*The Topper
Automatic Battery of Coffee Urns.*
They were the high tech
of their day, military
in their precision, dated
by a word that might have been
chosen from ancient Greece.

II.
At five a.m., last night's coffee
is a test of faith that might make one
who has known bitterness
wait for sunrise when the kitchen staff
arrives to make the coffee for breakfast.

But sometimes darkness is when
bitterness is best known for what it is,
and any coffee is better than the wait
for someone to come and make
coffee that has the taste of a new day.

III.
A cup of coffee carried
from the dining hall to a session
on suffering in the Bible
doesn't make it any easier
to swallow the stories of war
and sickness and disbelief
that build up to Jesus, himself,
on the cross wondering
how in the world God
can let such things happen.

But the cup is something
to hold onto, something that keeps
you from raising your hand
and telling your story. Your story
isn't Old Testament Job or Ruth;
but it's the kind of story that takes
cups and cups of coffee every morning
for you to make it out the door.

Finally, when the session is over
and people file out, you sit with the cup
empty, balancing it on your knee—
as if it's you, come to Holden
in hopes something said at vespers
or in a session or by someone
sitting on a porch will balance
the Old Testament and the New
into enough grace to refill
your cup again tomorrow morning.

Cute Maverick

There's that way she has of an innocent look
hiding the wrestling she did
as the only girl in a family with five brothers.
The times she followed to their games,
the door slammed against her hearing their talk
grew her up tough—but cute.
Now among young men thinking they need
to man up to find religion in the mountains,
that little girl look is her way of handling
overalls and beard in the wilderness.

The early ups and standing around to plan the day
put her where her brothers left her.
No one here will let her all the way in either;
so she smiles and outworks them,
leaves them behind when quick is needed,
remembers all the verses when Bible
on the porch after vespers is proof of faith.

They spend the summer at Holden pretending
equal in the work of the Lord. But after the wood
is chopped, the baggage loaded, the furniture moved,
when it's young men and a cute girl,
she stares them, *Don't*, with a look she learned
from the same look. When sitting close
on the porch at midnight might lead right back
to wrestling, and then beyond scripture,
she touches the hands away and goes to bed—
leaving them where she has so often been.

As If I Lived in the Old Testament

A boy of ten or eleven rounds the corner
on his way to get ice cream after vespers—
and crashes into me. I am down,
half knocked out, and he's just a boy
on the run who apologizes over his shoulder.
Stunned and a bit angry,
but unhurt, I watch him disappear
and chuckle at what I would have done
fifty years ago when I would have
taken the Lord's name in vain
and chased after that boy threatening to *kill you*.
As I get up, I notice a bush next to the sidewalk
turning red too soon for autumn—as if on fire.
Sitting on a branch, there is a bird
looking at me. No birder, I don't know its name;
but I know that if it sings
it will sound like the bush talking to me.

Fourth of July

The village wakes up ready for laughter,
then sets out on a day when anything
that comes to mind is America.
We dress in things brought from home,
found in the costume shop, borrowed
from a porch—hats and scarves, hiking boots
with a Speedo, masks and clown hair, flags
tied on sticks—strutted and pointed and laughed
from the time of the bell to start breakfast.

Morning proclamations and protests
shout to the mountains that Uncle Sam is no saint
and too often is too friendly with the devils
hiding in the details of government contracts
and secret reports. Prayers for peace
are scold and scripture with the faith of our fathers
needed now more than ever. Irreverent
and sacred and patriotic and angry and silly
go together in ways war memorials
and speeches back home cannot dare to tell.

The afternoon parade is loud longing
for all that is unnamed and full of tenderness
when small towns celebrate their ghosts.
The red, white, and blue that is expected
waves three-legged races and fire hose fights
and rhubarb pie on through to the evening—
then lowers its voice to talk of love.

The land of the pilgrim's pride is Biblical
in its proportion of goodness attempted,
and vespers tries to tell it so in a sermon
that preaches what it says in the *Declaration*—
and Luke. Love of country here rants
and raves and pokes fun through the day,
then sings the sacred so that tears matter.

At the evening concert, a piccolo
scavenged from copper tubing pinches *obbligato*
into the Sousa glory a little boy playing
on the floor turns to hear. The village is full
of those of us who come each year
for just this day; and we will smile with Jesus
and Jefferson mixed into the stories we tell
back home of the crazylove of God and country
celebrated on the Fourth of July at Holden.

In the mountains, fire works too well
for fireworks. So the day ends
in the village center with bubble wrap popping
in the dark as pictures of rockets and pinwheels
project on a screen set up to be the sky.
Hope files out the door afterwards
into the night where the new moon tries.
Watching it, wondering if America's flag
is still standing on the wilderness there,
we go to our rooms and pray goodnight.

Nursery Log

On a trail where old growth
defined the day,
herself in search of something new
in the difference
between stillness in the underbrush
and wind in the trees,
a nursery log
stopped her for an hour.

After a morning volunteering
in Narnia to help with the babies there,
the girl from Iowa,
come to Holden for a gap year
after four terrible years of high school,
needed wilderness
to be her caregiver;
and turning off the trail
where a nursery log waited,
careful not to disturb such beautiful rot,
she sat down to eat her lunch
and let nothing happen.

There beside her were mushrooms
and shoots of pine,
a blanket of moss, and ferns
growing out of the old log—
reminders of the time it takes
for wilderness to grow itself
from downfall
into the giant trees shading her.

Shadow of My Father

My father is in the garden again.
I assumed he was gone forever
after he collapsed behind the tool shed,
and I finished school and moved away.

Over the years, there has been no place
for growing anything.
It is work in big buildings.
It is small city lots.
Supermarkets are close by.

Stepping into a row of rhubarb
in the village garden
where I come each day to volunteer,
I kneel down the way he taught me,
the same as in church.

With the morning sun slanted
on my shoulder, there he is,
right beside me,
as if praying for my very soul.

The Cook's Birthday

It's his turn for the happy birthday song
at lunch, his choice of how to sing
the same old same old
so that it will give one minute of silliness
to the hours of doubt he has wrestled with
this whole year of volunteering to cook.

The hot and cold of his faith
was dangerous in the urban wilderness
around the big building he called church
at home. Here he has wished the simplest
of things—three meals, work, prayer,
hiking, reading, and time to sing and laugh.

He shouts for the song to be
à la Schwarzenegger. At the microphone
the request is repeated and treated
as gospel—and nonsense—
to be sung as if God is kicking his butt
and laughing great salvation.

Midnight Pilgrimage

There are places in the wilderness that eat light,
where darkness becomes a friend.
At Holden, the tailings, the gone baseball field,
the slope where Winston Camp is homeless,
those empty places give midnight a purpose—

to go there as everything disappears, wondering
what comes next, where to go when we leave here.
Going out looking for answers to questions
lingering from Bible study, from table talk at lunch,
is to journey to where Revelation waits.

The mountains cup the night down the valley
as if to tell the village lights *no chance.*
Flashlights get us across the walking bridge
to the tailings where a line of newly planted trees
guides us to Copper Creek.

Lying on the blankets we've brought,
looking up at the sky lighted by stars and hope,
we talk until dawn, dreaming answers
that guided saints and pilgrims home
from the edges of darkness they set out to find.

Volunteers

There is no salvation in escape
to wilderness after long walks
in city parks have not been enough.
Answers sought
to hearken heaven out of isolation
hold up only so long
as the wind is gentle
and the mountains keep to themselves.

Prayers brought from home
cannot be answered
by animals on the way
to high places up the trail.
Other wilderness pilgrims
can only respond
by keeping the same
loneliness to themselves.

Here, the girl in laundry who comes out
lesbian keeps her journal at night.
While cooking, the widower
daydreams about forty years no more.
Volunteers come for a month,
for a summer, for a year—
for the time it takes
Holden to answer their prayers.

GOING OUT

*It's the simplest and yet the fullest of all human
messages: "Good-bye."*

—Kurt Vonnegut in *Bluebeard*

Recycled Meditation

At a wilderness church camp, recycling
takes a scientific name. But *garbology* is religion too.
Boiled down to its simplest, we empty,
we sort, we crush, we bag, we haul,
we dump, we chop, we cover with sawdust and dirt.
Can we help but flash back to childhood
when grass clippings and weeds,
canned peaches gone bad, and table scraps
all went to compost behind the woodshed?

When the world was grownups,
the raising of children took chores, and the compost
went right back into the garden rows staked with string.
Recycling wasn't what we called it. Every day,
the bring it in, cook it, take it out, dump it,
turn and cover it was the way to make it
with one job, one car, one acre. It was the way
we wasted not, wanted not, the way
we helped God help those who help themselves.
Changing the oil every three thousand miles,
throwing change into a dish each day,
putting wood in for the winter were the same.
We did them religiously and learned they worked
the way giving cider time to harden was chemistry.

Now, forty years later, when science and scripture
both say the world needs saving,
we come to the wilderness each summer
where recycling makes good stewardship
the way one acre of chores simply made good sense.

Grownups

As the greatest generation
leaves the world behind,
the gray hair now coming to Holden
is their children—who first came here
when there was volleyball
after vespers, choose-up games
on the baseball field,
shirts and skins on the remains
of the concrete floor
of the mine's compressor room
still there for basketball on the third level.

Those days are still back home
in drawers of photographs.
Now a good book, conversation on the arc,
three sessions a day,
wine on the porch at dusk
is their recreation.
Ask them why they come;
but don't be surprised
if a smile and a long stare
up at the mountain peaks
is their only answer to such a question.

Sometimes All You Can Do Is Just Wonder

Tee-shirts sometimes say more than sermons.
That was the message. It didn't matter that there
was a sermon. What mattered was that the girl
giving the sermon last night at vespers was talking
with notes, but her tee-shirt was going off into
the space high up in the village center the way
fireworks go off in the sky ten miles north and you
wonder what they would look like if you were
right there. You want to see the last droop of fire
into the water. We couldn't take our eyes off
Religion sucks sometimes too. Couldn't. Didn't
want to. We wondered what set off that kind of
fireworks. Everyone gets to wear their version of
politics or love or football. But religion? Was she
just trying to be funny? She must have decided
God has something to do with broken hearts or
abuse or mean Twitter. But the woman knitting
in the first pew shook her head and speeded up.
A little boy in the back wondered if you can say
suck in church; and his mother, whose tattoo
under a short sleeve showed something about *love*,
explained with a hug. All of which leads you to
just wonder what it would have said if Mary had
been wearing a tee-shirt on the way to Bethlehem.

Jubilee

An old man sitting on the porch who has visited
Holden every year since 1965, says,

Let me tell you about what we called "Jubilee."
It was part of the hilarity that made Holden
Holden back in the day. But why would
anyone have gone to Leviticus? Too many laws.
Too many "thous" and "shalts." Too much God

stepping in like dads in charge of Little League.
It didn't happen every year. But Leviticus it was—
and when Holden needed to let go and play
and give back, up to the time the village closed
for mine remediation, it was Jubilee!

Always in July, it was a day when everything stopped
for the fun and games of it. Not much God
dropping by or anything Old Testament. But Jesus
all over the place and the Holy Ghost
doing a cakewalk. Then a silly-ridiculous auction

that brought Benjamin bids because everyone
was so moved. Like the M.C. at the talent show,
the picnic was full of baloney (some meat finally).
Ice cream sundaes for dessert for goodness sake!
In the evening, bread and wine, and a big sermon.

His eyes twinkle when he says that after Jubilee
at Holden, the stars shot across the sky like crazy.

Pure Darkness

At Holden, there is no city glow
on the horizon to damage the darkness.
Windows shine quietly enough
to do what's needed inside,
but don't pretend streetlights.
Porch lights left on
help to keep from stumbling
when someone sleepless or doubting
is up and on the way
to a place to read or pray.

Silhouette against the stars,
mountains keep the line
between heaven and here
where pure darkness is enough light
to know salvation
is wherever you find it—
at a wilderness retreat,
inside a lonely car,
on a park bench—and Sunday here
is every day of the week.

Holden Evening Prayer

Vespers in the wilderness
has to compete with awe,
and without music
might be just another way
to wind down the day.
That must have been
in Marty Haugen's mind
when in the winter of '86
he worked his music
into a divine twenty minutes
that ever since is his signature
at the bottom of evenings
everywhere—as John Hancock
as anything ever written
about the Holden Village
declaration that the Gospel
frees us from sin in the world.

Talk of Bread

The dining hall is full of the chatter
of, *What's for breakfast?*
The morning announcements
include a nonsense poem
to lend support to oatmeal, again,
and pancakes promised for later in the week.

The default is to bread toasted
and painted with peanut butter and jam,
with cinnamon and sugar, or butter and honey—
to sit on the plate beside the oatmeal
as some kind of morning dessert.

On Thursdays, lunch is as plain as monks eat
to remind us that the Third World
lives mostly by bread alone. When every day
someone whispers in the dinner line,
I wish I had a good hamburger,
here memory sometimes has to work at flavor.

The bread for breakfast, lunch, dinner,
and still there if needed for midnight,
is so much cliché it's joked into sermons
and scripture study to balance communion
with why we come to the wilderness.

We'll tell it as manna from heaven
as we try to explain back home
how a place of ministry,
often hilarious in its talk of holiness,
feeds the soul starving
for as much bread as can be baked.

Wilderness Psalm

1 It is the end of my last hike at Holden,
and I walk back to the village for dinner.
2 The trees that block the setting sun
have hidden in the valley a hundred years.
3 The wind has not reached them and
they are now giants.
4 Fire has burned them and let them
grow, burned them and let them grow.
5 Beneath them, the valley floor is full
of undergrowth tinder in the heat.
6 The weather report has warned, that
with lightening, fire will again cut through
brush and downfall like axes.
7 This valley is more metaphor than
I dare admit after this last week away
from the money and malls of my life.
8 I have walked this way to find
the peace of mind now walking with me.
9 The silence is reminder of all that I
came for, all that I have found.
10 At home, I will tell of what wilderness
teaches me and sing its praises.

Serious Stuff

When your core values try to include everything,
you had better deliver—and Holden does its best
at environment and social justice
and gender equity and diversity and ecology
and the kitchen sink
of what religion ought to be about
if God expects us to take care of his world.

The way it works in the village is not only
recycling and growing your own
and using downfall for heat and buying local
for food and volunteers to run the place;
it is also knowing that living in the wilderness
requires some of the old fashioned.

And even with *hilarity* as part of the promise,
those who have come the last five decades
know it is no joke to go for a hike, read on a porch,
attend a session on theology, worship,
talk in the dining hall, throw a pot,
keep a journal, or just sit and wonder—
they know the Gospel at work by being at Holden.

Tee-Shirt Cartography

Tee-shirts for sale in the bookstore
come in your favorite colors
with the village nestled
among the peaks ranged across the fronts.

Buckskin   Copper   North Starr   Martin Ridge
    Holden Village Dumbbell   Bonanza

map the horizon
where there is none.

Mountain valleys sometimes think
they have to have big, blue skies
and small towns with attitude.
Here the North Cascades
protect against too much sky,
and the village preaches beatitude.

So the tee-shirts keep it simple—
that names of the peaks
and the name of a church camp
are enough cartography for those
who have come to better understand
not to wear heaven on their sleeves.

Tuesday in the Bookstore

What do you need from a bookstore
     in the wilderness?
  You only brought one tee-shirt,
     but Potty Patrol has dozens.
You don't need a map; you can just follow the trail
     and then your nose.
You do need something sweet now and then,
    but there is always toast and honey
  in the dining hall.
    The souvenirs are tempting,
   but you never get the right ones.
 If you need to know about the mountains,
    you can go look.
You didn't understand the talk yesterday
  by the Chicago theologian,
     and his book costs $28.75.
You won't find any books about truth
  better than your old Bible.
 Postcards don't have enough room
     to describe paradise.
 A book about Holden? But you know
    the history of the village
  from when you were here
    three summers in the Eighties.
You brought three novels with you.
   You have soap. Bug spray.
But before you go out on the bus on Saturday,
    shouldn't you buy *something*?

A Volunteer's Good-Bye

On the last day, her farewell
is a poem and a prayer at matins
full of tears and her wilderness story.
The creeks and lakes of the mountains
have been baptism to her.
Her search for what's next
that had brought her to Holden
is over. She jokes of grace
found in the flavor of rhubarb pie.

Her two months are pressed
with dried flowers in her journal,
and the Holy Spirit is between the lines
she has written there.

She is packed and ready, she says,
for the trip down the mountain,
down the lake, back to home
where poems are rarely read
and tears seldom shed
with strangers. Hugs
and good-byes at the bus
will be *Amen*
to the prayer of who she came to be.

Go Tell It Down the Mountain

When you get back to the real world
and try to tell whoever will listen about Holden,
tell them you spent a week at an old mining town
the Lutherans got their hands on
and made into a place for holy talk, holy walk,
and Holy Cow! Tell them you went thinking
that without a TV or the internet there would be
nothing to do, but that you found
excitement just being in one place every day
doing the same things with the same people.
Tell them you went to all kinds of sessions,
they were called, where deep thinkers
got you talking about things
like forgiveness, like service, like salvation.
Tell them about the people you met—
and how six degrees of separation is more true
than all the clichés they've ever heard
because every day someone in the village
knew someone who knew someone
right back to you. Tell them how glaciers
and granite work together to grind beauty
down to just standing there in awe
at the overlooks on the trails along
Railroad Creek. Tell them hiking is religious,
not because it's such beautiful hiking,
not because it puts you in touch with spirits
told in Indian legends before God came along,
but because it hurts so good to do it
and treat it as pilgrimage in the wilderness.

Tell them that, never having been there before,
in one week you learned again
what all those good Lutherans
seem to know about places to visit
when vacation is religion.
Tell them there is rhubarb from the garden
every day. Tell them kids run far into the night
with their games. Tell them porches there
are confession and communion both.
Tell them that at prayer around the cross,
strangers pray for strangers as friends.
Tell them you raised your hand to volunteer
for dish team and laughed that
the Holy Spirit made you do it.
Tell of the soft, afternoon wind
that cools the trails through the big trees.
Tell the stories you were told about the old days
when it was a college kid who saved the place.
Tell the joke made in the sermon about Jesus
that was still the gospel truth. Tell them
Holden hilarity is good for the soul. Tell
how easy it is to speak up at book discussions
when you haven't even read the book—
and it's by a theologian who everyone
in the room seems to have as a neighbor.
Tell about the mountains and wilderness
in tales as tall as the trees
because Holden is as beautiful
as any place this side of the Promised Land.

Tell them at Holden you might find the Holy Spirit
going to the end of the road
in the middle of nowhere,
going to meals with strangers
who are just as nervous about what to say as you,
going to vespers every night
and pretending at songs you've never sung,
going for hikes along trails
that look down on nothing but down,
going to sleep in a place so quiet deer eating
at the lawns in the morning wake you,
going past the snack bar in the afternoon where
if you stop someone will offer to buy you ice cream,
going down the mountain and people sending you off
with a wave good-bye that means every word
of the prayers they've said for your safe travel home.

Departure

The liturgy of departure is always the same.
Breakfast and packing and luggage set out
fill the final morning,
followed by a kind of wake
when there is nothing to do but sit.
Maybe visit the bookstore.
Find something to read in the library.
Take a short walk down by the river.
It all slows down to memories.

The bell that rings to start each day
signals the end now—five times loud and then
drifting back to silence as if to soothe reality.
From around the village people come to the bus
where we wait for someone to hug us
and wish us well. Exaggeration hides the heartfelt,
and laughter promises staying in touch.
It's the same as yesterday and every day
that requires chapter and verse to carry on.

As we leave, we remember the hikes we took,
the day we volunteered for dish team,
the time we paused to marvel
at a five-year-old loose in nature.
The journal we kept is full of notes
about prayer and laughter mixing,
service instead of just sitting there,
the hike we took to heaven on earth, at Holden,
a holy ghost town, a metaphor in the mountains.

EPILOGUE

Postcard to Holden

Just a note to say thanks. Got back
to the world yesterday. Unpacking,
found a handout from a nature walk.
Couldn't remember all the names of things
along the way. Doesn't matter.
Words everyone used on the walk tell it all.
Green. Unspoiled. Remote. Grand.
Serene. Quiet. Peaceful. Glorious.
At every turn, a kid in front kept saying,
Holy Cow! Look at that!
A place that needs its own thesaurus.
Guy from Minnesota maybe said it best,
God, it's beautiful.
Might have been a prayer.

> Glad you are there

A Brief Chronology

15,000 B.C.	The glaciers of the North American ice age gouge out the fifty-five-mile trench that will become today's Lake Chelan, the third deepest lake in the United States
8,000 B.C.	The last glaciers down to the lake melt while glaciers on the North Cascade peaks continue to send water down to the lake
In the 1880s	The Great Northern and Northern Pacific railroads explore possible routes through the Cascades along what will come to be known as Railroad Creek
In the 1890s	J.H. Holden begins prospecting in the Railroad Creek Valley and files a claim on what is today Copper Mountain
In the 1920s	After Holden's death in 1918 and efforts by others to develop the claim, the Howe Sound Company leases the claim and begins work to develop the Holden Mine
1937- 1957	The Howe Sound Company operates one of the largest copper mines in the country and maintains the town of Holden to house 400 miners and their families
1957- 1960	The mine closes, the town is left empty, and Wes Prieb, a student at the Lutheran Bible Institute in Seattle, writes letters inquiring about the ghost town which is for sale
October, 1960	The mine, its structures, and the town of Holden is "sold" to LBI for one dollar and the land on which the village stands is leased from the US Forest Service

Early 1960s	LBI students and church volunteers work to clean up and restore the town, and today's Holden Village opens to guests as a Lutheran retreat center in 1962
In its first years	The village's core values—worship, theology, hospitality, vocation, diversity, grace, shalom, ecology, gifts, study, rest, place, community, and hilarity—are established
1960s-2012	Holden operates as a retreat center that welcomes 4000-5000 visitors a year from all religious faiths, all parts of the world, and all kinds of backgrounds
2013-2016	The village is closed to summer guests while work is done to seal the mine shaft, capture the contaminated water draining from it, and build a water treatment plant
Summer 2017	After five hundred million dollars is spent by the multinational Rio Tinto Group to do the mine remediation work, Holden reopens with full summer and winter programs
2017-today	Although much has changed around the village with new roads, new buildings, infrastructure work done to update power and water systems, Holden the village remains very much as it was when abandoned and what it became as a retreat center that continues to welcome all who come seeking what the wilderness offers

Identification of Terms and Places

The Arc: A raised, circular deck at the center of the village for informal gatherings and meetings

The Baseball Field: Originally a full-sized baseball field used by Holden miners, then used by villagers for pick-up games, now an empty open space

The Bell: Located on the arc, a large bell rung to indicate times for meals and scheduled events

The Bookstore: A combination bookstore, post office, shirt shop, reading room, and a place to get trail supplies, toiletries, village art, or a candy bar

Chalet Hill: Fourteen houses on the hill above the main buildings of the village where permanent staff and teaching staff live

The Costume Shop: A room where clothes left behind at Holden are stored for anyone to use for dress-up

The Garden: For many years a large garden was maintained at Holden to supplement the locally grown food brought in; now the garden grows mostly rhubarb and flowers

Holden Evening Prayer: Originally entitled *Vespers '86* when written by Marty Haugen at Holden for evening worship, now widely known as *Holden Evening Prayer* still used for vespers in the village and widely among Lutheran congregations

Jubilee: The Old Testament celebration every 50th year told of in the book of Leviticus

The Lady of the Lake: One of two boats, known as the slow boat, that brings visitors up Lake Chelan to Holden

The Lakes: Besides Lake Chelan, the lakes to which Holden visitors hike are Image, Lyman, Holden, Hart, and Domke, with Image Lake the longest hike at 36 miles round-trip and Hart Lake the shortest at 9 miles

Lucerne: In the days of the mine, a village on Lake Chelan where the copper ore was shipped out; now the place where arriving visitors leave the boat to start the bus ride up the eleven miles to Holden Village

Maverick: A volunteer assigned to woodcutting, luggage transport, furniture moving, and odd jobs

The Mountains: The mountains around Holden are named Buckskin, Copper, North Star, Dumbbell, Bonanza, with Martin Ridge rising behind the village

The Museum: Originally a stand-alone building with mine artifacts and wilderness information, then torn down in the way of mine remediation, now temporarily housed in the upstairs of the village center

Narnia: The nursery at Holden where parents can leave toddlers and infants each morning

Potty Patrol: A term used for the place for lost and found and where things left by visitors are kept for anyone to take

Prayer Around the Cross: A service with seating configured around a cross on the floor during which worshippers are invited to come, kneel at the cross, light a candle, and pray

Rio Tinto Group: The multinational mining company that was mandated to pay for mine remediation after having bought other mining companies and the liability for the contamination created by the Howe Sound mine at Holden—with 500 million dollars spent to do the work of clean up as of 2018

Snack Shop: During the days of the mine, a small lunch counter/soda fountain in the village center; now where ice cream is served in the afternoon and evening

The Tee-Shirt: Holden is known for the tee-shirt that has the five mountains that rise around Holden printed across its front with the village name nestled among them

The Third Level: The term used in the early days of the village where the mine portal opened onto tracks leading to the old buildings where the ore separation process had been done

The Village Center: The old gymnasium converted into the village worship center above with the pool hall, bowling alley and game room in the basement

Volunteers: There are a number of paid permanent staff at Holden, but most of the work is done by volunteers who come for a minimum of two or three weeks and a maximum of . . .

Winston Camp: The name used to refer to the one hundred homes that housed married miners and their families—and were destroyed by the Forest Service when LBI assumed ownership of Holden

About the Author

Tim Sherry is a husband and father, a grandfather and great grandfather. He was a high school teacher and coach and principal. He earned a B.A. in English from Pacific Lutheran University and an M.A. in English from the University of Chicago. He has lived in Chicago and for a short time in Europe, has traveled widely throughout the United States, but has always called Tacoma, Washington home.

For most of his life, he kept his writing private with only a few attempts at publication. But with the support of poets in the Auburn, Olympia, and Tacoma writing communities, since 2002 he has had poems published in *Rattle, Crab Creek Review, Cirque, The Broad River Review, The Raven Chronicles*, and others. He has been a Pushcart nominee, had his poetry recognized in contests, and in 2010 was an Artsmith Artist Resident on Orcas Island. *One of Seven Billion*, his first full-length poetry collection, was published by MoonPath Press in 2014.

timsherry@comcast.net

From the Author

Holy Ghost Town began in the summer of 1967 when I
and my wife, Marcia, visited Holden Village not long
after it had opened as a Lutheran retreat center. We
and our family have visited and volunteered there many
times since, and in 2009 and 2010 the first poems in this
collection were born—and added to during the Artsmith
residency. Over the next year, the poems grew
into a chapbook that was a finalist in the 2011 Flying
Trout chapbook contest.

Since then, with much thanks to Elaine Harrison and
Larry Howard at Holden, Peter Ludwin, Allen Braden,
and Connie Walle of the Puget Sound Poetry
Connection, Janet Grant, former director at Holden,
and Marcia at home, the poems have been added to,
rewritten, and organized in the hope that they reflect
what one might experience during a week in July spent
in the Railroad Creek Valley where Holden Village, just
being there, is a kind of miracle.

About CIRQUE PRESS

Cirque Press grew out of *Cirque*, a literary journal established in 2009 by Michael Burwell, as a vehicle for the publication of writers and artists of the North Pacific Rim. This region is broadly defined as reaching north from Oregon to the Yukon Territory and south through Alaska to Hawaii – and east to the Russian Peninsula. Sandra Kleven joined *Cirque* in 2012 working as a partner with Burwell.

Our contributors are widely published in an array of journals. Their writing is significant. It is personal. It is strong. It draws on these regions in ways that add to the culture of places.

We felt that the works of individual writers could be lost if they were to remain scattered across the literary landscape. Therefore, we established a press to collect these writing efforts. Cirque Press (2017) seeks to gather the work of our contributors into book-form where it can be experienced coherently as statement, observation, and artistry.

Sandra Kleven – Michael Burwell, publishers and editors

cirquepressaknw@gmail.com
www.cirquejournal.com

Books by **CIRQUE PRESS**

Apportioning the Light by Karen Tschannen (2018)

The Lure of Impermanence by Carey Taylor (2018)

Echolocation by Kristin Berger (2018)

Like Painted Kites & Collected Works by Clifton Bates (2019)

Athabascan Fractal: Poems of the Far North by Karla Linn Merrifield (2019)

Holy Ghost Town by Tim Sherry (2019)

Drunk on Love: Twelve Stories to Savor Responsibly by Kerry Dean Feldman (2019)

Seward Soundboard by Sean Ulman (2019)

Silty Water People by Vivian Faith Prescott (2019)

More praise for *Holy Ghost Town*

In *Holy Ghost Town*, Tim Sherry tells the story of a place in the wilderness that is much more than beautiful landscape. In words clear and full of tenderness, he describes an abandoned mining town turned into a Lutheran retreat center that I and all who go there know as a place of reflection and transformation. Sometimes he puts words to what I have felt and couldn't express on my own. Other times he sheds light on something I have seen differently or not at all. It is poetry in which I can lose myself and find myself. Sherry's poetry reflects balance between faith and doubt, escape and reality, history and hyperbole, the serious and hilarious, that all who have been there know to be Holden Village, "a holy ghost town, a metaphor in the mountains."

> — Elaine Harrison, long time assistant to the
> directors at Holden Village

The story of Holden Village told in Tim Sherry's *Holy Ghost Town* is one you might call serendipitous, though the visitors who come each year to the old mining town, now an ecumenical Christian retreat center in the north Cascades, know it as a place to shed worries, make room for peace of mind, marvel at the beauty of God's wilderness, and live the core values of the Holden community. It is a stirring history of the grand dreams, the love of wilderness, and faith in God that every morning herald a bright new day when one out hiking at Holden might imagine being "right at heaven's door" around the next bend in the trail.

> — Marjorie Rommel, 2016-17 Auburn
> poet laureate

Made in the USA
Middletown, DE
02 August 2019